To _____ Katie _____

From _____ Fotini _____

My Favorite Recipes:

Hope you Enjoy

these Floridian

recipies

with love
Fotini

Signed _____

Date _____

Printed in the United States of America on acid-free paper

Library of Congress Catalog Card Number: 2009909767
ISBN 978-0-9760555-3-2

Cover and book designer: Susannah Green
Cover illustrations: Hannah Bureau
Illustrations: Kathy Taylor Zimmerman (herbs), Hannah Bureau (flamingos)

SEASIDE PUBLISHING

Seaside Publishing is a division of the University Press of Florida.

For a complete list of Seaside books, please contact us:
Seaside Publishing
15 Northwest 15th Street
Gainesville, FL 32611-2079
1-352-392-6867
1-800-226-3822
orders@upf.com
www.seasidepublishing.com

Easy Breezy
Florida Cooking

Joy and Jack Harris

Seaside Publishing
Gainesville/Tallahassee/Tampa/Boca Raton
Pensacola/Orlando/Miami/Jacksonville/Ft. Myers/Sarasota

CONTENTS

Introduction

Appetizers

Salads

Entrees

Sides

Soups, Stews and Sandwiches

Desserts

Our Love Affair...
With Food

Call it a love affair with food: My cooking, Jack eating — each of us doing what we love. So it seems only natural that when we met for the very first time it was in a kitchen. The kitchen was in a television studio. Jack was the show's host. I was there to teach viewers how to cook Florida seafood. Talk about an easy job!

Not only am I crazy about Florida seafood, I'm crazy about all things "Florida," including a West Virginia transplant, my husband, Jack Harris.

My passion for cooking began as a child in my mother's kitchen where her much-used red-checkered cookbook became one of my favorite things to read.

I have fond memories of family reunions. Reunions where farm-fresh eggs and vegetables from the garden were served alongside all my aunts' scrumptious homemade cakes and pies. This was the education of my senses —the basis for my appreciation of fresh, wholesome, delectable food.

Today, most of my cooking is influenced by the amazing foods we have in abundance here in Florida. Fresh-from-the-water seafood, Ruskin tomatoes, Florida sweet onions, juicy Zellwood corn, mammoth Plant City strawberries, fragrant Cuban bread, sweet orange blossom honey, tart Key limes, mouth-watering oranges, heavenly blueberries, ripe avocado, guava and more.

If you are from Florida, or a neighbor, and have access to these flavorful and locally grown products, choose them above all else! They will make a vast difference in your cooking. If you don't happen to live in Florida, shop at markets that import these foods in season, and if you can't find them, find the freshest and best available wherever you are. Remember that great cooking starts with great ingredients.

I have been cooking for many years and still bake my traditional Christmas gingerbread men with the same recipe I used while I was in high school. In college, I majored in Home Economics. After

teaching six years, I took a new career path working for the state of Florida, endorsing our bountiful seafood both here and abroad.

A number of recipes in this book (recipes by me, comments by Jack) are years-old favorites. Some are new, but all are easy-to-prepare and even easier to eat.

Joy

Postscript by "Cracker" Jack Harris

As a radio and television show host in Florida for more than 30 years, I have had the opportunity to taste cuisine from around the globe. I always found interviewing cooks and chefs a fascinating aspect of my job. Watching them prepare wonderful food was one of the best things I got to do.

For several years I worked as a restaurant reviewer and on a weekly basis I tried many new dishes and usually loved them all. Clearly, I have a passion for eating and I have been lucky enough to be in the right profession to indulge that passion.

I've been more than lucky to have a wife who is as skilled as Joy is in the kitchen and I am thrilled that she is sharing her talent and her recipes with you. My contribution to this book is as an appreciative audience — which, she assures me, is no small thing for a cook. I tasted every dish and provided some commentary on each. But let me say this: it was the best job I ever had.

APPETIZERS

Tampa Bay Black Bean Relish

Did this dish spawn the word "relish" as a synonym for savoring something? From whence cometh the word "relish" in the first place? Did someone once "lish" a food, and when it was brought out as a leftover, "lished" it again, hence, they "re-lished" it?
—Jack

1 (15-ounce) can black beans, drained and rinsed
¼ cup sweet pickle relish
½ cup apple cider vinegar
2 tablespoons sugar
1 tablespoon lime juice
½ teaspoon salt
½ teaspoon pepper
¼ teaspoon ground cumin
¼ cup chopped sweet onion

- Place beans and pickle relish in a large mixing bowl with an airtight lid. Set aside.
- In a small saucepan, combine vinegar, sugar, lime juice, salt, pepper and cumin. Bring to a boil, then lower heat and simmer for 1 minute.
- Add onion to saucepan and continue cooking 2 to 3 minutes more.
- Pour vinegar and spice mixture over black beans and relish.
- Toss lightly, cover and refrigerate several hours or overnight.

Servings: 4 to 6

Guava Glazed Cinnamon Sausage Gems

My wife says this recipe will make 30 appetizers, which would be good for 30 tiny people, but if you love these things as I do, you'll get about 4 or 5 servings, maybe fewer. They're great with beer or other beverage of choice. —Jack

4 ounces medium Cheddar cheese (see Note)
½ pound hot ground sausage
1 cup all purpose flour
1 teaspoon cinnamon
2 tablespoons guava jelly

- Preheat oven to 400 degrees F.
- Grate the cheese and bring it and sausage to room temperature. Mix sausage with flour and cinnamon. Mix in cheese. Form sausage mixture into 1" balls and place in a single layer on a 15"-by-10" baking sheet. Place in the oven and bake for 12 minutes.
- Meanwhile, in a small saucepan, melt the jelly over medium heat. Keep warm. Remove sausage balls from oven. Drizzle with melted jelly. Serve with wooden picks.

Yield: 30 appetizers

Note: *Do not be tempted to substitute sharp or extra sharp Cheddar, as they tend to be drier than medium Cheddar. And do not buy pre-shredded cheese. Pre-shredded cheese has an ingredient that keeps it from sticking together.*

Citrus Bruschetta

The Italian word "bruschetta" means "toast" or "burn," which is what you do to the bread. But Joy's recipe calls for Cuban bread, so it might more aptly be called Citrus Tostada. Although it looks Italian, it's more akin to our Cuban/Florida heritage.   —Jack

2 large ripe tomatoes, seeded and chopped
Juice and zest of 1 lemon
Juice and zest of 1 orange
2 tablespoons light olive oil
1 teaspoon sugar
½ teaspoon salt
¼ teaspoon pepper
¼ teaspoon allspice
½ loaf Cuban bread, cut crosswise about ½" thick

- Combine all ingredients except bread in a medium mixing bowl with a tight fitting lid. Chill several hours.
- Preheat oven to 375 degree F.
- Toast Cuban bread slices until golden, turning once or twice as it bakes.
- Using a slotted spoon and draining tomato mixture well, spoon about 1 tablespoon of tomato mixture on top of each bread slice. Serve.

Servings: 24

Sunshine Scallop Skewers

I love scallops prepared in just about any fashion, but this is my favorite. The tender meat is actually a muscle, as opposed to a mussel. Specifically, it's the big, meaty abductor muscle that we eat. Scallops can reach the ripe old age of 18 years, unless, of course, they are caught and eaten, and this recipe gives good reason why they should be. —Jack

12 sea scallops
2 tablespoons extra virgin olive oil
Juice and zest of 1 lime
Juice and zest of 1 orange
2 cloves garlic minced
½ teaspoon ginger
¼ teaspoon salt

- Combine all ingredients in a resealable plastic bag and shake to coat scallops evenly. Chill about 30 minutes.
- Remove scallops and place 3 on each of 4 skewers taking care to insert skewers through the thickest part of the scallops. Prepare gas or charcoal grill. Place skewers over medium-high direct heat for 2 to 3 minutes per side.

Servings: 4

Creamy Shrimp Dip

It's the dip that's creamy, not the shrimp. My wife claims it serves 6, but that's a matter of taste, and the shrimp size — and shrimp size is a term to ponder: How can you have "large shrimp?" Seems oxymoronic! —Jack

1½ pounds cooked, peeled and deveined shrimp
¾ cup whipped cream cheese
1 tablespoon mayonnaise
1 teaspoon Worcestershire sauce
1 clove garlic, minced

- Chop shrimp and combine with remaining ingredients in a medium-size mixing bowl.
- Chill.
- Transfer to a serving dish and surround with carrots and celery sticks or crackers.

Servings: 6

Cuban Bread Pizza with Roasted Tomato Sauce

Had Marco Polo gone east not west in his travels, and found his way to Cuba instead of China, this might have been the recipe he brought back to Italy. Too bad the Italians missed out on great dishes such as this one made with Cuban bread. —Jack

1/3 loaf Cuban bread (about a 12" section)
Roasted Tomato Sauce (recipe follows)
1 cup shredded mozzarella cheese

- Preheat oven to 450 degrees F.
- Slice the bread lengthwise.
- Spoon desired amount of sauce on cut side of bread. Top with cheese.
- Place on an ungreased baking sheet and bake about 8 minutes or until cheese starts to bubble. Remove from oven.
- Using a pizza cutter, cut the pizza into 1½" wide pieces.

Servings: 4 to 6

Recipe continues on next page ⊃

Roasted Tomato Sauce

6 large ripe tomatoes, cored, seeded and chopped
½ cup minced sweet onion
3 cloves garlic, minced
2 teaspoons sugar
1 teaspoon salt
¾ teaspoon pepper
½ teaspoon crushed dried oregano
2 tablespoons extra virgin olive oil

- Preheat oven to 450 degrees F.
- Combine tomatoes, onion, garlic, sugar, salt, pepper and oregano in a large ovenproof Dutch oven.
- Stir in olive oil.
- Roast, uncovered for about 30 minutes. Remove from oven and mash with a potato masher. If the mixture is too thin, cook longer on the stovetop, over medium-high heat, until reduced to the desired thickness.

Yield: about 2½ cups

Easy Florida Guacamole

Never a big fan of guacamole, I learned to love it, especially this version of it, when we had bountiful avocado trees in our backyard. We replaced them with oak trees, but when Joy tried to use acorns in the recipe instead of avocados, it was a dismal failure.

—Jack

1 large ripe avocado (see Note)
2 tablespoons Key lime juice
2 cloves garlic, minced
1 teaspoon salt
½ teaspoon red pepper flakes
¼ teaspoon ground cumin

- Cut avocado in half, remove seed and scrape avocado into a large bowl, mash with lime juice, garlic, salt, pepper and cumin.

Servings: 4 to 6

Note: *To tell if an avocado is ripe, flick the stem. If it snaps off easily, it's ready to be used.*

Gators-in-a-Blanket

This perfect Florida appetizer remotely resembles a tiny alligator all wrapped with its tail sticking out. In spite of the name — PETA please take note — not a single piece of alligator is used. Such cleverness and tastiness deserves a cheer: "Two bits, four bits, six bits, a dollar ... all for Gator Tails, stand up and holler!" —Jack

24 pods pickled okra
24 slices white bread
4 ounces whipped cream cheese, room temperature
¼ cup butter, melted

- Preheat oven to 400 degrees F.
- If okra pods are moist, pat dry with paper towels.
- Remove crusts from bread and discard. Flatten remaining bread with a rolling pin. Spread each slice with cream cheese and place an okra pod on each. Let tip of pod extend beyond the bread edge. Roll up bread around pod.
- Place on greased baking sheet, seam side down and brush with melted butter. Bake for 8 to 10 minutes.

Yield: 24 gator tails

Kumquat Salsa

My wife tells me the humble kumquat is a dichotomy. Though it looks like a runt orange, it has a sweet peel and a tart center. She says if you use only the peel, it lends a light citrus flavor. It's the secret ingredient in this delightful salsa variation.   *—Jack*

2 kumquats, inside removed and minced (see Note)
1 large tomato, seeded and diced
2 tablespoons chopped sweet onion
Juice of 1 lime
1 clove garlic, minced
1 tablespoon dark brown sugar
½ teaspoon salt
⅛ teaspoon allspice
Dash cayenne pepper
Toasted Cuban bread slices
2 kumquats sliced and seeds removed, optional garnish

- Mix together all ingredients, except for the bread and kumquats for garnish, in a large mixing bowl.
- Cover and refrigerate mixture for several hours or overnight.
- Serve on top of thinly sliced and toasted Cuban bread. Garnish serving platter with remaining two kumquat shells.

Yield: about 1 cup

Note: *Cut kumquat in half lengthwise and remove insides by turning shell inside out. Discard inside and mince skin.*

Cocktail Olives

Although these olives are technically a garnish for a martini, Joy likes to serve them as an appetizer. They are good enough to stand on their own, and the best part is that you don't have to drink martini after martini to get to the olive. At least, I think that's the best part. —Jack

1 (10-ounce) jar pimiento-stuffed olives
3 tablespoons fresh squeezed lemon juice
1 teaspoon lemon zest
1 tablespoon red wine vinegar
1 clove garlic, minced
¼ teaspoon crushed dried oregano
⅛ teaspoon crushed red pepper

- Drain about ⅓ cup liquid from olives in the jar; set aside.
- Mix together lemon juice, zest, vinegar, garlic, oregano and pepper in a measuring cup with a spout. Pour mixture back into olive jar. Fill remaining space with reserved olive juice.
- Screw the top back on the jar and shake well.
- Refrigerate and marinate about a week before serving.

Yield: about 2 dozen

Lemon-Spinach Mushrooms

To me, a "mushroom" is where you play "Post Office" at a party. I like that idea a whole lot better than actual mushrooms, but I love this recipe. I'm convinced you could make lemon-spinach baseball caps, and they'd taste wonderful if they were made with this recipe. —Jack

**1 (10-ounce) package frozen, chopped spinach
1 (6-ounce) package Baby Bella mushrooms, ends trimmed
1 tablespoon extra virgin olive oil
Juice and zest of 1 lemon
¼ cup minced sweet onion
½ teaspoon salt
⅛ teaspoon pepper**

- Cook spinach according to package directions; drain well. Place in medium size mixing bowl; set aside.
- Remove stems from mushroom caps and chop fine. Reserve caps. Heat olive oil in a large skillet with a lid. Add mushroom stems, lemon zest and onion; sauté about 4 to 5 minutes. Add mushroom mixture to spinach and mix.
- Put mushroom caps in a skillet, topside down. Saute 2 to 3 minutes.
- Spoon spinach mixture into mushroom caps, then cover and cook over medium-low heat 5 to 6 minutes more.
- Remove cover and sprinkle with lemon juice, salt and pepper.
- Using a slotted spoon remove the mushrooms from the accumulated liquid in the pan.

Yield: about 2½ dozen

Mango Meatballs

In my humble gustatory opinion, these are fabulous. I am not alone in my conclusion. It is also the consensus among our guests. My wife usually has these delicious tidbits simmering on the stove as company arrives. With the toothpicks stationed nearby, it's easy for guests help themselves. The meatballs disappear in a very short time. —Jack

2 cups mango jam
1 ½ cups chili sauce
2 tablespoons lemon juice
1 pounds lean ground beef
½ pound ground pork
½ cup crushed cornflakes
2 eggs, slightly beaten
⅓ cup ketchup
2 tablespoons chopped fresh parsley
2 tablespoons soy sauce
1 clove garlic, minced
1½ teaspoons salt
½ teaspoon pepper

- In a large saucepan, combine mango jam, chili sauce and lemon juice. Bring to a low simmer over medium heat and stir well until blended.
- Combine beef, pork, cornflakes, eggs, ketchup, parsley, soy sauce, garlic, salt and pepper in a large bowl.
- Mix well and form into 1½" balls; place in mango sauce mixture.
- Stir gently to coat meatballs with sauce.
- Cover, then simmer slowly for about 45 minutes.

Yield: about 3 dozen meatballs

Shrimp with Honey Cocktail Sauce

This sauce is so good it would make just about anything taste better. I'll bet that even little chunks of liver would be palatable dipped in this sauce. I could just eat the sauce, and I would, too, but that would be insensitive to the shrimp.   —Jack

1 tablespoon orange blossom honey
½ cup ketchup
½ cup chili sauce
1 tablespoon horseradish
1 tablespoon apple cider vinegar
2 pounds shrimp, cooked, peeled and deveined

- In a medium-size mixing bowl, combine honey, ketchup, chili sauce, horseradish, and vinegar.
- Mix well to blend flavors; chill.
- Serve in a small bowl surrounded with chilled shrimp for dipping.

Servings: 6

Tropical Nachos

Our son Jackson, who obviously did not get his kitchen talents from me, created this snack. You might say he's "nacho" chip off the old block. His spice preference is Old Bay® Seasoning, though you may desire something else. Feel free. —Jack

6 8" flour tortillas
2 teaspoons Old Bay® Seasoning
Kumquat Salsa, drained, (see page 10)
4 ounces Monterey Jack cheese with
jalapeno peppers, grated
1 cup Easy Florida Guacamole (see page 8)

- Preheat oven to 350 degrees F.
- With a pizza cutter or sharp knife, cut each tortilla into 8 even triangles. Place triangles on a large ungreased baking sheet. Sprinkle with seasoning blend.
- Bake until crisp, about 15 minutes. Top with salsa and grated cheese; bake an additional 3 to 5 minutes.
- Remove chips from pan to serving platter before they begin to stick to the pan. Serve with guacamole.

Servings: 4 to 6

Ybor City Cheese Toast

Ybor City Cheese Toast is fine any time — at breakfast, as an appetizer or a dinner accompaniment. It's so easy to make and yet it delivers such a tremendous taste. I like it broiled a little longer than most, until the edges are dark and crispy. —Jack

¼ loaf Cuban bread, sliced lengthwise
2 tablespoons butter
4 ounces shredded Cheddar cheese

- Preheat broiler for 10 minutes.
- Spread butter on inside of each slice of bread. Top with grated cheese.
- Place on a broiler rack. Broil 3" from the source of heat for 4 to 5 minutes.

Servings: 6

SALADS

Florida Stars
Chicken Salad

Carambola is another name for "star fruit." I love the word "carambola." It sounds like an invective, as in, "Carambola! That is one good looking piece of chicken!" No one ever mistook the word "pineapple" for an invective. —Jack

2 cups chopped, cooked chicken breast
1 Red Delicious apple, cored, peeled and diced
1 teaspoon lemon juice
½ cup mayonnaise
1 teaspoon soy sauce
½ teaspoon curry powder
2 star fruits, sliced

- In a large bowl, toss chicken and apple with lemon juice
- In a small bowl, combine mayonnaise, soy sauce and curry. Pour over chicken mixture and toss again. Serve chilled on sliced star fruit.

Servings: 4 to 6

Note: *The star fruit is completely edible but you may want to trim any brown edges before slicing.*

Sunny Day Chicken Salad with Lime Dressing

The finest demise for leftover chicken is chicken salad. I like tuna salad better than chicken salad, but this recipe closes the gap. I wonder what tuna would taste like in this recipe. For that matter, it might make for a great beef salad, or even a pork salad. In fact, why doesn't anyone make a pork salad? After all, it is the other white meat. —Jack

1 cup finely chopped cooked chicken
1 (3-ounce) package cream cheese at room temperature
¼ cup ripe olives, chopped
2 tablespoons mayonnaise
1 tablespoon lemon juice
½ teaspoon salt
¼ teaspoon white pepper
1 bunch romaine lettuce, washed and torn into bite-size pieces
2 carrots, washed, peeled and shredded
Lime Dressing (recipe follows)

- Mix together chicken, cream cheese, olives, mayonnaise, lemon juice, salt and pepper. Set aside.
- Toss lettuce with carrots and divide among four salad plates. Top each bed of lettuce with ¼ of the chicken mixture and drizzle with Lime Dressing.

Servings: 4 to 6

Recipe continues on next page ⊃

Lime Dressing

Juice and zest of 1 lime
½ cup sour cream
1 tablespoon honey
1 teaspoon grated fresh ginger

- In a bowl, whisk together lime juice, zest, sour cream, honey and ginger.

Yield: about ¾ cup

Citrus and Stars

This dish is about as "Florida" as you can get, with homegrown carambola (star fruit), grapefruit, oranges and juice from limes. All are indigenous. We also have bees, so we get honey, too, though it aggravates the bees to no end. It's not difficult to tell Florida bees from out of state bees. Florida bees have their little left blinker on all the time.   *—Jack*

1 star fruit, sliced crosswise (see Note 1)
1 grapefruit, peeled and sectioned
3 oranges, peeled and sectioned (see Note 2),
juice reserved
3 tablespoons honey
2 tablespoons Florida orange juice
1 tablespoon lime juice

- Place the star fruit, grapefruit and orange segments in a bowl. Set aside.
- Whisk together honey, orange juice and lime juice.
- Pour over citrus segments. Toss and Chill.

Servings: 4 to 6

Note 1: *Also known as carambola, star fruit is most plentiful in the fall and winter.*

Note 2: *When you peel and section the oranges, reserve 2 tablespoons of juice to use in the recipe.*

Summer Sky Greek Salad

This is our obeisance to Tarpon Springs, our gastronomically rich Greek community in the Tampa Bay area. After a rough day of sponge diving, there's no better way to start a meal than with this Greek salad. Or, if you're eating a little light, it becomes the meal itself. —Jack

1 head iceberg lettuce, washed and torn into bite-size pieces
2 tomatoes, seeded and chopped
1 cucumber, peeled, seeded and chopped
½ cup crumbled feta cheese (see Note)
1 small green bell pepper, seeded and chopped
2 radishes, thinly sliced
12 kalamata olives
12 green olives
Greek Dressing (recipe follows)

- Toss the lettuce and tomatoes, cucumber, cheese, bell pepper, radishes, and olives in a large bowl. Pour Greek Dressing over salad; toss again.

Servings: 4 to 6

Note: *Feta cheese is a traditional Greek cheese usually made from sheep or goat's milk and stored in its own salty whey or brine. It is available in ethnic food stores and supermarkets.*

Recipe continues on next page ⊃

Greek Dressing

½ cup white vinegar
½ cup light olive oil
1 teaspoon dried oregano (see Note)
1 teaspoon dry mustard
1 teaspoon salt
½ teaspoon pepper

- Mix all ingredients in a jar with a tight fitting lid and shake well.

Yield: about 1 cup

Note: Greek oregano is an especially aromatic and recommended for this recipe. It can be found in Greek or Middle Eastern food stores.

Frosty Florida Fruit Salad

This is one of my favorites, and if it didn't have that big old cup of sugar, it would actually be a health drink. But keep the sugar in because that is what makes it sensational! And, despite the sugar, this salad is a great way to get kids to eat their fruit. Same for big kids like Joy and me. —Jack

**4 cups freshly squeezed Florida orange
juice (divided use)
1 cup sugar
Juice of 1 lemon
2 cups very thinly sliced strawberries
1 banana, sliced**

- Place 1½ cups orange juice and sugar in saucepan; bring to a boil over medium-high heat.
- Reduce heat and simmer rapidly for 12 to 14 minutes until it is reduced to a syrupy consistency.
- Remove from heat and cool. Add remaining orange juice and lemon juice. Stir in strawberries and bananas.
- Pour mixture evenly into six 10-ounce containers with lids for the freezer. Freeze, stirring or shaking containers every 30 minutes for 1½ hours or three times. This will help distribute the fruit.
- Thaw slightly in the refrigerator for about 30 minutes before serving.

Servings: 6

Lemon Whip Fruit Salad

Contrary to the old saw, "If it tastes good, it ain't good for ya," this terrific treat is chock full of vitamins as well as great refreshment in hot weather. There may be some who are concerned about the name "lemon whip." It is a bane to folks who feel that the poor helpless lemon should not be abused. For them, we'll call it Lemon Timeout Fruit Salad. —Jack

1 banana, sliced
1 teaspoon lemon juice
3 cups strawberries, stems removed and sliced
¾ cup blueberries
Lemon Whip (recipe follows)

- Toss banana and lemon juice in a bowl, toss in strawberries and blueberries. Serve with dollop of Lemon Whip.

Servings: 6

Lemon Whip

½ cup chilled whipping cream
2 teaspoons lemon juice
1 teaspoon lemon zest
2 teaspoons sugar

- Whip cream, juice, zest and sugar in a very cold bowl until soft peaks form.

Yield: about 1 cup

Hot Lime Slaw

Everything about Lime Slaw is terrific except the name. The word "slaw" is strange. It's a word that when repeated ten or twelve times becomes almost deviant. And then when you add the word lime to it, there's the "sl" from slaw, and the "ime" from the lime and... aw forget about it... —Jack

2 slices bacon
¼ cup chopped sweet onion
3 cups thinly sliced cabbage
3 medium carrots, peeled and shredded
1 clove garlic, minced
¼ cup soy sauce
Juice of 1 lime
1 teaspoon sugar
½ teaspoon dry mustard
⅛ teaspoon pepper

- Fry bacon in a 10" skillet until crisp. Remove from pan with a slotted spoon. Drain on paper towels. Crumble and set aside. Reserve drippings.
- Sauté onion in bacon drippings over medium-high heat, until tender.
- Add cabbage and carrots, stir; reduce heat, cover and cook about 6 to 8 minutes.
- Transfer to a serving bowl.
- In same skillet, add garlic and sauté about 1 minute. Stir in soy sauce, lime juice, sugar, mustard and pepper; bring to a boil and cook for 1 minute. Pour over cabbage mixture. Sprinkle with reserved bacon. Serve warm.

Servings: 4 to 6

Note: *The slaw can be refrigerated and then reheated briefly in a microwave. Toss again before serving.*

Orange Grove Romaine Salad

The pièce de résistance in this recipe is the Honey Mustard Dressing. Joy points out that one of the keys to getting just the right flavor is to use Hellmann's® Mayonnaise, which is OK by me. But then my son would prefer using Heinz® Ketchup; in his opinion, anything tastes better with ketchup. I'm with Joy on this one.   —Jack

1 bunch romaine lettuce, washed, dried and torn into bite-size pieces
2 oranges peeled and sectioned
2 tablespoons grated Parmesan cheese
Honey Mustard Dressing (recipe follows)

- Place romaine, orange segments and Parmesan cheese in a large bowl; toss ingredients lightly. Serve with Honey Mustard Dressing.

Servings: 4 to 6

Honey Mustard Dressing

½ cup mayonnaise
1 tablespoon honey
1 tablespoon spicy brown mustard
2 tablespoons lemon juice

- Place all ingredients in a medium-size mixing bowl; whisk together until thoroughly blended.

Yield: about ¾ cup

Red Leaf Salad with Cuban Croutons and Maple Dressing

Cuban bread is so delicious that we rarely have any left over to make croutons. But when we do, this is the dish for them. The salad gets an additional flavor spike from the combination of maple syrup and balsamic vinegar in the sumptuous dressing. It can be best described as a kind of Vermont and Verona mind meld.

—Jack

**1 bunch red leaf lettuce, washed, dried and torn into
bite-size pieces
Cuban Croutons (recipe follows)
Maple Dressing (recipe follows)**

- In a large salad bowl, toss lettuce with croutons and serve with Maple Dressing.

Servings: 4

Cuban Croutons

**¼ loaf Cuban bread, cut into ½" cubes
2 tablespoons extra virgin olive oil
2 large garlic cloves, peeled and crushed
¼ teaspoon salt**

- Preheat an oven to 350 degrees F.
- Combine bread, oil, garlic and salt in a large, resealable plastic bag. Seal shut and shake to coat bread cubes.
- Spread cubes on a large, rimmed baking sheet; bake about 10 minutes or until golden.

Servings: 4 to 6

Recipe continues on next page ⊃

Red Leaf Salad with Cuban Croutons and Maple Dressing

Maple Dressing

3 tablespoons maple syrup
3 tablespoons balsamic vinegar
3 tablespoons extra virgin olive oil
1 tablespoon grated onion
¼ teaspoon dry mustard
¼ teaspoon salt
¼ teaspoon white pepper

- Place all ingredients in a jar with a tight fitting lid.
- Shake well, until thoroughly blended.

Yield: about ¾ cup

Taste of Florida
Tomato-Lime Salad

My son and I thought that tomato sauce on pasta and ketchup were the ultimate uses of the tasty and healthful tomato, but this tomato dressing takes the prize. I wonder how it would taste on spaghetti or french fries? —Jack

10 cups mixed salad greens, washed dried and torn into bite-size pieces
2 large ripe tomatoes, each cut into 8 wedges
1 large sweet onion, thinly sliced
Tomato-Lime Dressing (recipe follows)

- Toss greens with tomatoes and onion in a large salad bowl. Serve with Tomato-Lime dressing.

Servings: 4 to 6

Tomato-Lime Dressing

⅓ cup tomato sauce
⅔ cup light olive oil
⅓ cup apple cider vinegar
Juice of 1 lime
1/3 cup sugar
¼ teaspoon salt

- Place all ingredients in a jar with a tight fitting lid.
- Shake well, until thoroughly blended.

Yield: about 2 cups (This is more than you will need, but it can be kept in the refrigerator for other uses.)

Spinach Salad with Mushrooms and Manchego Cheese

I'm not wild about spinach, simply because of the grit that clings to my teeth when I bite in. A scientist friend says it's the mineral salts from the oxalic acid in the spinach that actually coats teeth, but I just call it "spinach fuzz" and I could live without it. As for the Manchego cheese – I don't know a thing about it, except it's Spanish and it saves this salad. —Jack

6 ounces baby spinach, washed, stems removed
4 ounces white mushrooms, thickly sliced,
stems removed
4 ounces Manchego cheese, grated
Sweet and Sour Dressing (recipe follows)

- Place spinach, mushrooms and cheese in a large bowl and toss.
- Serve with Sweet and Sour Dressing.

Servings; 4 to 6

Sweet and Sour Dressing

½ cup ketchup
¼ cup honey
¼ cup light olive oil
2 tablespoons apple cider vinegar

- Place all ingredients in a jar with a tight fitting lid.
- Shake well, until thoroughly blended.

Yield: about 1 cup

Strawberry Orange Garden Salad

The citrus industry would be wise to manufacture and market this orange dressing. Hey, Misters French® or Kraft® or Heinz® ... are you listening? How does Joy's Orange Dressing sound? Nah ... "the Joy of Dressing" sounds like a fashion show.   —*Jack*

**2 heads Bibb lettuce, washed and torn into
bite-size pieces
½ cup strawberries, stems removed and sliced
½ cup Orange Dressing (recipe follows)
Freshly ground black pepper**

* Toss together lettuce and strawberries in a large salad bowl. Drizzle with Orange Dressing. Sprinkle with pepper to taste.

Servings: 4 to 6

Orange Dressing

**½ cup orange juice
½ cup sugar
¼ cup light olive oil
1 tablespoon yellow mustard
¼ teaspoon salt**

* Place all ingredients in a jar with a tight-fitting lid. Shake until thoroughly blended.

Yield: about 1¼ cups

ENTREES

Ruskini Aurora

Our favorite tomato-producing town in Florida is Ruskin. The beautiful tomatoes grown there were the inspiration for this pasta dish that we named "Ruskini" which combines "Ruskin" with "rotini," the famous Italian pasta recognizable by its shape of twists and spirals that embrace both refined and simple sauces.

—Jack

2 tablespoons olive oil
¼ cup minced sweet onion
2 medium cloves garlic, minced (about 2 teaspoons)
¼ teaspoon red pepper flakes
3 large tomatoes, cored, seeded and chopped
½ cup tomato juice
1 teaspoon Worchestershire sauce
½ teaspoon salt
½ cup heavy cream
8 ounces rotini pasta, cooked according to package directions and kept warm
½ cup freshly grated Parmesan cheese

- Heat oil in a large saucepan over medium heat. Add onions and sauté about 3 minutes.
- Add garlic and pepper flakes; cook about 1 minute more.
- Stir in tomatoes, tomato juice, Worcestershire sauce and salt; simmer for 25 to 30 minutes, stirring occasionally, until most of the liquid has evaporated.
- Stir in cream and heat thoroughly. Add warm pasta, stir and serve with Parmesan cheese on the side.

Servings: 6

Sunshine State Shrimp Kebobs

This is such a terrific way to fix shrimp, it even makes mushrooms taste good. This is pushing it, because I'm not a big mushroom eater. Instead of four shrimp and four mushrooms per skewer, just make it eight shrimp, but that means three people would have no shrimp and six mushrooms. The key is to keep the guest list 50 percent vegan. —Jack

24 large shrimp, peeled and deveined
¼ cup freshly squeezed orange juice
2 tablespoons soy sauce
2 tablespoons light olive oil
½ teaspoon salt
24 button mushrooms, ends trimmed

- Combine shrimp, orange juice, soy sauce, oil and salt in a resealable plastic bag and marinate about 15 minutes in the refrigerator.

- Drain marinade and discard. Alternate shrimp and mushrooms on 6 skewers starting with a shrimp and ending with a mushroom.

- Prepare grill for direct heat cooking. Place skewers on grill rack that has first been sprayed with non-stick cooking spray. Grill over hot coals or gas heat for 4 to 5 minutes per side or until shrimp turn from translucent to white.

Servings: 6

Floridian
Oven-Fried Grouper

I think this is the best grouper recipe ever, although there are seafood purists who don't think fish should be crunchy, but that's probably because they haven't tried this dish. Once sampled, you'll understand where the term "groupie" comes from. I'm certainly one of them.
                                                                    —Jack

2 pounds grouper fillets
1½ teaspoons salt (divided use)
½ cup buttermilk
½ cup crushed corn flakes
½ teaspoon Old Bay® Seasoning
2 tablespoons butter

- Cut fillets into serving-size portions and sprinkle with 1 teaspoon of the salt.

- Soak fillets in the buttermilk for about 30 minutes; drain fillets, discard the milk.

- Combine cornflakes with Old Bay® Seasoning and the remaining salt. Roll fillets in the cornflake mixture and place in a buttered baking pan. Dot each fillet with a pat of butter.

- Place pan under a preheated broiler for 10 to 12 minutes or until fish flakes easily when tested with a fork.

Servings: 4 to 6

Snapper au Gratin

Anything can be made palatable by administering copious amounts of cheese. Even a potholder becomes edible. But when you add cheese to an outstanding piece of fish such as snapper, it is doubly wonderful. If you are really a big cheese lover, you might add a lot of cheese, and make "Gratin au Snapper." —Jack

4 snapper fillets
2 tablespoons butter, melted
1 teaspoon salt
1 teaspoon pepper
1 (5-ounce) can evaporated milk
1 cup Cheddar cheese, grated

- Arrange fish in a well-buttered baking dish; brush with butter and sprinkle with salt and pepper. Preheat broiler for 10 minutes. Broil fillets 3 inches from source of heat for about 8 minutes (see Note).
- Pour milk over fish and sprinkle with cheese
- Broil until cheese melts and fish flakes easily when tested with a fork, about 4 minutes.

Servings: 4 to 6

Note: *Cooking times vary according to thickness of fish. Usually 10 minutes for every inch of thickness.*

Chicken and Yellow Rice

This is an Ybor City staple, and though I may be prejudiced, I think Joy's chicken and yellow rice is as good or better than anything this side of The Columbia. That's the restaurant, not the river. But then, The Columbia is more than a hundred years old — Joy is considerably younger.   *—Jack*

1 (5-ounce) package yellow saffron rice
1 pound boneless skinless, chicken tenderloins
1 teaspoon salt
¼ teaspoon pepper
2 tablespoons olive oil
½ cup chopped sweet onion
1 medium red bell pepper, seeded and chopped
2 cloves garlic, minced
1½ cups water
1 (10-ounce) package frozen baby peas, thawed

- Preheat oven to 375 degrees F.
- Sprinkle chicken with salt and pepper.
- Heat oil in a 3½ - to 4-quart heatproof Dutch oven over medium-high heat. Add chicken, turning often until lightly brown on both sides (browning should take about 3 to 4 minutes).
- Push chicken to one side; add onion, bell pepper and garlic; cook, stirring often until vegetables are tender (about 4 minutes).
- Stir in yellow rice and water; bring to a boil. Remove from stovetop and place in the oven; bake, covered for 15 minutes.
- Remove from oven and add peas. Return to oven and bake an additional 15 minutes or until chicken is done (juices should run clear).

Servings: 4 to 6

Curry Lime Chicken

Curry gives this recipe the taste of India and the lime gives it zing. But then is "zing" a culinary word? If Colonel Sanders had put this on the menu, he'd have had to change his name to "Raja" Sanders.
—Jack

1½ pounds skinless, boneless chicken beast
Juice of 3 limes
¼ cup maple syrup
2 tablespoons extra virgin olive oil
2 cloves garlic, minced
1 teaspoon curry powder
1 teaspoon salt

- Place chicken in a large re-sealable plastic bag. Add lime juice, syrup, oil, garlic, curry powder and salt.
- Seal bag and shake to distribute marinade evenly over chicken.
- Refrigerate for at least 4 hours or overnight.
- Preheat broiler for 10 minutes. Remove chicken from marinade. Discard marinade. Place chicken on a broiler pan that has been sprayed with non-stick cooking spray. Place broiler pan 2 inches from the source of heat. Broil for 8 to 10 minutes on each side.

Servings: 4 to 6

Kumquat Chicken Kebobs

The name "kumquat kebab" is alliterative and fun to say. It would make a great name for a clown on kids' TV. The combination that makes this dish so special is soy, vinegar and honey. If you don't like the kumquats, you can just eat every other piece. If you don't like the chicken, you're un-American.   —Jack

24 kumquats
1 pound chicken tenders
¼ cup soy sauce
2 tablespoons water
1 tablespoon balsamic vinegar
1 tablespoon honey
1 tablespoon extra virgin olive oil
1 clove garlic, minced

- Wash kumquats. Set aside.
- Cut chicken tenders into 20 bite-size pieces and place in a heavy duty resealable plastic bag with soy, water, vinegar, honey, oil and garlic.
- Reseal bag and shake to distribute ingredients evenly over chicken.
- Place in refrigerator for at least 1 hour to marinate.
- Drain chicken. Discard marinade. Thread chicken pieces alternately with kumquats on 4 skewers, beginning and ending with kumquats. Grill over hot coals for 10 to 12 minutes per side, turning skewers often so that the chicken cooks uniformly.

Servings: 4

Orange-Onion Chicken Sauté

The orange adds a certain sweetness to this dish, making it a chicken recipe worth crowing about. Did you ever wonder where the name "orange" came from? And which came first, the color or the fruit? And if it had the color of orange (so they called it that), why weren't grapes called "purples", and cherries called "reds"?
—Jack

4 boneless, skinless chicken breast halves
2 tablespoons olive oil
Juice and zest of 1 orange
1 sweet onion, sliced
2 cloves garlic, minced
½ teaspoon salt
¼ teaspoon pepper

- Trim excess fat from chicken breasts, rinse and pat dry.
- In a large heavy skillet, heat oil over medium heat. Sauté chicken in the oil for about 3 to 4 minutes on each side.
- Add the orange juice, zest, onion, garlic, salt and pepper. Cover and cook until chicken is done, about 5 minutes more.

Servings: 4

Florida Herb-Grilled Turkey Breast

Florida fresh herbs make grilling an epicurean adventure. Two of the most common herbs here are rosemary and thyme, which Joy uses when grilling turkey. All I know about them I learned from Simon and Garfunkel's "Scarborough Fair." The rest is pure "Joy." Thyme is highly aromatic with a spicy taste, and rosemary's distinctive pine flavor goes well. —Jack

2 tablespoons chopped fresh rosemary
Zest of 1 lemon
½ teaspoon sea salt
¼ teaspoon black pepper
1 tablespoon olive oil
1 (3-pound) boneless turkey breast

- Mix rosemary, zest, salt, pepper and oil in a small bowl. Rub on turkey breast, being sure to cover entire surface.
- Prepare or preheat grill. Place a drip pan in the middle of charcoal or beneath where turkey will cook on a gas grill. Oil the grill rack. When coals are ready, or gas grill is at the correct temperature, place turkey, skin side up, on the grill rack.
- Cover grill, leaving vents open. Roast to an internal temperature of 170 degrees F. on a meat thermometer, between 1¼ and 1¾ hours.
- When done, remove from grill, cover in foil and allow to rest about 20 minutes. During resting time, the turkey will continue to cook as juices settle in the meat.

Servings: 6

Citrus Rubbed Steak

A Texan might be appalled at the sub-tropical taste given to his southwestern cows, but if he took one bite, he'd agree that the seasoning gives an old-fashioned steak a unique and zesty flavor. And besides, Florida cattlemen would understand and applaud this innovative step. If a Texan still has a beef with this, tell him to eat it! —Jack

Zest of 1 orange, 1 lime, 1 lemon
2 teaspoons ground coriander
2 teaspoons paprika
2 teaspoons dark brown sugar
1 teaspoon ground cumin
1 teaspoon dry mustard
1 teaspoon ground ginger
1 teaspoon fresh ground black pepper
1 teaspoon salt
4 rib-eye steaks, each 1" thick

- Mix together all ingredients except the steaks in a small mixing bowl.
- Spread mixture evenly on steaks, rub in.
- Refrigerate steaks for several hours to allow the rub to adhere to the steak.
- Place steaks on an oiled grill rack 3 inches above hot coals or source of heat. Cook turning once, until desired degree of doneness. For rare, cook 3 minutes on one side; turn and cook for 4 more minutes. For medium, cook 4 minutes, turn, and cook for 5 minutes more. For well done, cook for 5 minutes, turn, and cook for 6 minutes more.

Servings: 4

Note: To determine if charcoal is hot enough, hold your hand over the coals, palm side down. If you can keep it there for only 2 seconds, the temperature is high or hot enough.

Grilled Filet Tips with Fontinella Fondue

I ate this for dinner the night before I wrote this note, so the flavors were still vivid in my mind. To put it succinctly: It is a gustatory delight beyond compare. The filet was excellent — credit to the cow. But when dipped in Joy's fontinella cheese sauce, it was elevated to a new level. Fontinella cheese, also called fontina cheese, is a cow's milk cheese with a memorable tang.   —Jack

1 pound filet mignon, cut into 1" pieces
2 tablespoons olive oil
2 cloves garlic, minced
½ teaspoon salt
¼ teaspoon pepper
2 sweet onions, each cut into 4 wedges
Fontinella Fondue (recipe follows)

- Put beef cubes in a heavy-duty resealable plastic bag along with olive oil, garlic, salt and pepper. Reseal the bag and shake to distribute ingredients evenly over beef. Chill about 1 to 2 hours. Bring meat to room temperature before cooking.
- Remove beef from marinade. Discard marinade. Alternate filet tips with onion wedges on 4 to 6 skewers.
- Grill over direct heat 3 to 4 minutes on each side.
- Serve with Fontinella Fondue for dipping.

Servings: 4 to 6

Recipe continues on next page ⊃

Fontinella Fondue

8 ounces fontinella cheese, shredded
1 large egg yolk, beaten
1 cup heavy cream

- Heat cream in a 2-quart saucepan over medium-high heat until boiling. Gradually whisk in egg yolk. Reduce heat to low, continuing to whisk until the cream and egg yolk are slightly thickened. Remove from source of heat, then add cheese and stir until melted.

Yield: about 2 cups

Orange Cream
with Tenderloin

This dish is a magnificent reflection of our state's cuisine. It pairs one of our favorite citrus products with one of our very tasty cows. The tenderloin tastes great, but the orange cream sauce makes it something extra special, and very much Florida. —Jack

1 (3- to 5- pound) beef tenderloin roast
1 tablespoon extra virgin olive oil
¼ teaspoon pepper
¼ teaspoon salt
Orange Cream Sauce (recipe follows)

- Preheat oven to 425 degrees F.
- Place tenderloin on rack in a shallow roasting pan, then tuck smaller end of tenderloin under the rest of the loin to even it out.
- Rub with olive oil then sprinkle with pepper and salt.
- Roast, uncovered, about 15 minutes per pound. (Meat thermometer should read 140 degrees F.)
- Remove from oven and cover with foil. Let stand for about 15 minutes. Serve with Orange Cream Sauce.

Servings: 4 to 6

Orange Cream Sauce

Juice and zest of 1 orange
1 cup sour cream
2 teaspoons horseradish

- Combine all ingredients in a medium-size mixing bowl. Chill.

Yield: about 1½ cups

Lemon-Lime Chops

I love the taste that soy sauce adds to the chops. Joy recommends marinating 2 hours or overnight, I urge you to do so overnight because the longer they marinate, the more the sauce soaks in, and the richer the flavor. —Jack

Juice and zest of 1 lime
Juice and zest of 1 lemon
½ cup soy sauce
¼ cup extra virgin olive oil
2 cloves garlic, minced
¼ cup orange blossom honey
6 boneless pork chops, each 1" thick

- Whisk together juices, zest, soy, olive oil, garlic and honey.

- Place chops in a heavy duty, resealable plastic bag. Seal bag, marinate in the refrigerator for at least 2 hours, or overnight.

- To prepare grill: Set up grill with hot coals on one side and medium hot on the other.

- Remove chops from marinade. Discard marinade. Place chops on an oiled grill rack over hot coals and cook 2½ minutes per side to sear in juices.

- Move chops over medium-hot coals and cook 8 to 10 minutes per side.

Servings: 6

Slice of Heaven
Orange-Glazed Ham

The orange glaze gives this ham a unique tangy sweetness. It will leave you with a deep appreciation of orange syrup and a question that remains to be answered: Why doesn't the citrus industry bottle an orange syrup? Great over ham, but also buttered flapjacks. —Jack

1 (5- to 7-pound) fully cooked semi-boneless ham
1 small orange, thinly sliced
¼ cup honey
½ cup fresh squeezed orange juice
½ teaspoon ground cloves

- Preheat oven to 325 degrees F.
- Place ham on rack in open roasting pan. Insert meat thermometer into center of meat. Bake 20 minutes per pound or until thermometer reaches 140 degrees F.
- Meanwhile, combine honey, juice and cloves in a saucepan. Simmer about 15 minutes until the mixture is reduced to a syrupy consistency.
- Remove ham from oven 30 minutes before end of cooking time; cut off any tough outer skin and discard.
- Brush with juice mixture; finish cooking while brushing with mixture every 10 minutes. Before the last 10 minutes of cooking, arrange orange slices over ham and brush with remaining juice mixture. Use a wooden toothpick, if necessary to secure orange slices to the ham.

Servings: 8 to 10

Sweet Orange Rubbed Pork

My wife tells me that the difference between rubbing the pork and marinating it is that the marinade penetrates the entire piece of meat, not only altering the taste, but tenderizing it as well, while the rub merely adds flavor to the outside. We know people enjoy getting massages; perhaps they might also enjoy getting marinated. —Jack

1 teaspoon orange zest
½ teaspoon salt
½ teaspoon pepper
¼ teaspoon cinnamon
2 pounds pork tenderloin
1 tablespoon vegetable oil
¼ cup maple syrup

- Sprinkle zest, salt, pepper and cinnamon over tenderloin; rub in and let sit for about 20 minutes.
- Preheat oven to 400 degrees F.
- Heat oil in a large skillet over medium-high heat. Brown tenderloin in skillet for about 1 minute on each side, using tongs to turn the meat.
- Transfer tenderloin to rimmed baking sheet and pour maple syrup in skillet. Simmer about 4 minutes, stirring and loosening brown bits in the pan. Cool slightly, then drizzle over pork.

Recipe continues on next page ⊃

Sweet Orange Rubbed Pork

- Place tenderloin in oven for about 30 minutes or until internal temperature reaches 145 degrees F. Remove from oven and cover loosely with foil for 5 to 10 minutes, while internal temperature reaches 160 degrees F. (see Note).

Servings: 6

Note: *The meat continues to cook even after it is removed from the oven. By allowing the covered pork to rest a few minutes after cooking, the internal temperature reaches a higher degree. If you leave the pork in the oven until it reaches 160 degrees F., it will continue to cook to an even higher temperature once it is removed and it will over cook and become dry and tough.*

SIDES

Cinnamon Sugar Grapefruit

Grapefruit is terrific for your health, but this recipe turns the ordinary grapefruit into a GREATfruit. The heavy sweet coating might diminish the health benefits of our citrus pride, but it certainly enhances the taste. And, it might encourage kids to take a sample. You know what they say about a spoonful of sugar. —Jack

3 grapefruit
3 tablespoons unsalted butter, melted
3 tablespoons light brown sugar
½ teaspoon cinnamon

- Preheat broiler for 10 minutes.
- Cut each grapefruit in half and loosen each section.
- Combine butter, sugar and cinnamon in a small bowl. Spread ⅙th of the mixture over each cut side of the grapefruit.
- Place on a 15"-by-10" baking sheet, cut side up and broil for about 5 minutes, until top is bubbly.

Servings: 6

Collard Greens
Florida Style

*If you're from the backhome of Florida or the hills of West Virginia,
as I am, you know that "collards" or "greens" are a diet staple (FYI:
No Cracker calls collard greens by both names at the same time).
The old recipe was basically to slather them in bacon grease. This
recipe elevates greens to semi-gourmet status.*   —Jack

**1 pound frozen, chopped collard greens
2 slices bacon
1 onion, chopped
1 red bell pepper, seeded and diced
2 cups chicken stock
1 cup water
1 tablespoon sugar**

- Cook bacon in a 10"-frying pan until crisp. Remove from pan with a slotted spoon. Drain on paper towels. Crumble and set aside.
- Sauté onion and bell pepper in bacon drippings until soft, about 4 minutes.
- Bring chicken stock and water to a boil in a large saucepan or 3-quart Dutch oven.
- Add collard greens, bacon, onion-pepper mixture and sugar to stock. Bring to a boil. Cover, lower heat and simmer for 45 minutes to an hour.

Servings: 4 to 6

Cuban Garlic Bread

Here's a way to turn Cuban bread into an hors d'oeuvre by slicing it into serving-size pieces with a pizza cutter. At Thanksgiving and Christmas, Joy sprinkles poultry seasoning on the bread instead of pepper and it tastes even more festive. I personally prefer to heat the bread long enough to get the edges crispier. But then, I'm a little weird. —Jack

½ cup butter, melted
¼ cup grated Parmesan cheese
4 cloves garlic, minced
1 tablespoon lemon juice
¼ teaspoon salt
½ loaf Cuban bread, sliced lengthwise
¼ teaspoon white pepper

- Preheat oven to 425 degrees F.
- Combine butter, Parmesan cheese, garlic, lemon juice and salt.
- Place bread slices, cut side up, on baking sheet and spoon butter mixture over all. Sprinkle with pepper. Heat for 10 minutes.

Servings: 4 to 6

Ginger-Orange Asparagus

I personally love asparagus when it's grilled, but this indoor ginger-orange recipe is almost as good as the al fresco version, plus the microwave is far more convenient than the grill, unless you have a really old, old microwave that requires lighter fluid and a match to get it started. I jest! —Jack

1 pound fresh asparagus, ends trimmed
Juice and zest of 1 orange
1 teaspoon freshly grated ginger
¼ teaspoon salt
¼ teaspoon pepper

- Place the asparagus in microwave-safe dish.
- Sprinkle evenly with orange juice, zest, ginger and salt. Cover with clear plastic wrap leaving one corner loose to allow steam to escape. Microwave on HIGH 6 to 8 minutes.
- Sprinkle with pepper.

Servings: 6

Ginger-Orange Carrots

No offense to Bugs Bunny but carrots have been anathema to me. However, this recipe makes them palatable. The more ginger and orange juice, butter, salt and pepper, the better, I always say.   —Jack

**1 pound carrots (about 6 medium), peeled and cut
into ½" rounds
1" piece fresh ginger, peeled and cut into 4 pieces
½ cup water
½ teaspoon salt
¼ cup orange juice
1 tablespoon butter
1 tablespoon sugar
⅛ teaspoon pepper**

- Bring carrots, ginger, water and salt to boil in a 2-quart saucepan over high heat; reduce heat to medium and simmer until carrots are almost tender, about 7 minutes.
- Add orange juice, butter, sugar, and pepper to simmering carrots and bring to a boil, stirring constantly; cook for about 7 minutes.
- Remove ginger with a slotted spoon; drain carrots and serve.

Servings: 4 to 6

Deeper than Deep South Hoppin' John

This is the traditional Southern New Year's dish said to bring good luck. There are various explanations for the origin of the name "Hoppin' John," but the most plausible is that it came from a similar Caribbean dish that, in French, was called "pois a pigeon," with "pigeon" pronounced something like "pwahahpeejawng," which somehow the English picked up as "Hoppin' John."

—Jack

8 ounces dried black-eyed peas
8 cups water, divided use (see Note)
4 slices bacon
1 medium onion, chopped
1 green pepper, seeded and chopped
1 cup white rice
1½ teaspoons salt

- Rinse peas in cold water, taking care to remove any foreign particles.
- Soak peas overnight in a 3-quart saucepan with enough water to cover 1 inch over the peas (about 4 cups).
- Drain peas and add fresh water, enough to cover about 1 inch above peas (again, about 4 cups). Bring to a boil; reduce heat and simmer, uncovered, about 1½ hours. Stir occasionally.
- Meanwhile, cook bacon in a heavy frying pan over medium-high heat until crisp. Remove bacon from pan. Drain on paper towels. Set aside.

Recipe continues on next page ⊃

Deeper than Deep South Hoppin' John

- Add chopped onion and green pepper to frying pan and sauté in remaining bacon drippings until tender, about 5 minutes over medium heat.
- Add onion mixture, crumbled bacon, rice and salt to the peas. Stir well to combine. Reduce heat to medium and simmer, covered, about 30 minutes more.

Servings: 6

Note: *Water and times are approximate in this recipe. All the water should be absorbed by the final cooking time.*

Lime Broccoli

The most presidential aspect of my son's makeup is his disdain for broccoli, just like the 41st President, George H. W. Bush. I think that's a function of kids... to disdain broccoli. I hated it as a child and referred to it as "trees." Unlike George H. W. Bush, I learned to like it as an adult, especially when spiced up a little as it is in this recipe.   *—Jack*

2 cups broccoli florets
Juice of 1 lime
1 teaspoon extra virgin olive oil
¼ teaspoon salt
¼ teaspoon pepper

- Place broccoli in a microwave-safe dish and sprinkle with lime juice, olive oil and salt. Cover with clear plastic wrap, leaving one corner loose to allow steam to escape. Microwave on HIGH 4 to 5 minutes. Sprinkle with pepper.

Servings: 4 to 6

Limed Spinach

Popeye never knew what he was missing! Just a few minor adjustments and a dish of spinach becomes an epicurean delight so lush that even Bluto would have craved it. Oh, but then who would have won their epic battles? —Jack

1 (9-ounce) bag spinach, washed, dried, stems removed
1 teaspoon lime juice
1 tablespoon extra virgin olive oil
2 cloves garlic
¼ teaspoon salt
¼ teaspoon pepper

- Place olive oil and garlic cloves in a large microwave-safe dish and then cover.
- Microwave on HIGH 1 to 2 minutes until garlic is soft. Add spinach, sprinkle with lime juice, cover, and microwave 1 to 2 minutes more. Stir, season with salt and pepper.

Servings: 4 to 6

Orange Roasted Apples

This is a terrific breakfast dish along with eggs, grits, burnt toast and burnt bacon, and it's an equally delightful accompaniment to pork at dinnertime. With apologies to the old saw, "an apple a day keeps the doctor away," — "an orange a day makes the apple a day taste better." —Jack

1 green apple such as Granny Smith, cored, peeled and cut into eighths
1 Red Delicious apple, cored, peeled and cut into eighths
Juice and zest of 1 orange
1 tablespoon light brown sugar
½ teaspoon cinnamon
⅛ teaspoon salt
1 tablespoon butter

- Heat oven to 400 degrees F.
- Toss apples with orange juice, zest, brown sugar, cinnamon and salt in an 8"-by-8" baking dish. Dot evenly with butter.
- Place in the oven and bake for 30 minutes.

Servings: 4 to 6

Oven Fries with Zesty Orange Catsup

Oven fries are a terrific substitute for traditional french fries, but when enhanced by hot orange catsup, they're even tastier. Purists like my son will tell you it's impossible to improve on nature's perfect food – catsup – but this is a spicy alternative. Personally, Jackson and I prefer the orange catsup with guava jelly rather than hot pepper jelly. —Jack

4 medium baking potatoes, washed, dried, peeled and cut lengthwise into thin strips
4 tablespoons extra virgin olive oil (divided use)
2 teaspoons coarse salt (divided use)
Freshly ground black pepper to taste
Zesty Orange Catsup (recipe follows)

- Preheat oven to 450 degrees F.
- Coat a 17"-by-11" rimmed baking pan with 1 tablespoon olive oil and then sprinkle evenly with 1 teaspoon of the salt. Place potatoes in a large resealable plastic bag with remaining 3 tablespoons oil, remaining salt and pepper. Seal bag and shake to evenly coat potatoes. Spread potatoes in a single layer over the salted pan. Bake about 15 minutes.
- Remove from oven and turn potatoes over. Continue baking about 15 minutes more or until golden brown.
- Serve with Zesty Orange Catsup.

Servings: 4 to 6

Recipe continues on next page ⊃

Zesty Orange Catsup

½ cup ketchup
2 tablespoons hot pepper jelly (see Note)
Juice and zest of 1 orange (about ¼ cup of juice)

• In a 1-quart saucepan, cook together ketchup, jelly,
  orange juice and zest, stirring well to blend ingredients.
  Simmer about 5 minutes. Cool before serving.

Yield: ¾ cup

Note: For a sweeter rather than hot taste, substitute guava jelly.

Quick Parmesan-Lemon Asparagus

Hey! What's the hurry, Joy? If you like asparagus, you'll love this au gratin treatment. Again, it's the cheese factor. Sprinkle a little Parmesan on it and a piano key will taste pretty good. So you can imagine what it will do to asparagus. It tastes just great! So take your time to enjoy. —Jack

**1 pound fresh asparagus, ends trimmed
2 tablespoons water
1 tablespoon lemon juice
2 tablespoons grated Parmesan cheese
¼ teaspoon salt
¼ teaspoon pepper**

- Place the asparagus in a microwave-safe dish.
- Sprinkle with water, lemon juice, Parmesan cheese, salt and pepper.
- Cover with clear plastic wrap leaving one corner loose to allow steam to escape. Microwave on HIGH 6 to 8 minutes.

Servings: 6

Rosemary
Roasted Potatoes

Who in the heck was Rosemary after whom this herb was named? And who in the heck was Herb after whom this Rosemary was named? Rosemary - the herb — was once a substitute for frankincense, which means that the Wise Men could have come bearing gifts of gold, rosemary and myrrh. But I digress. Rosemary in this recipe tastes great. —Jack

4 Yukon Gold potatoes
16 sprigs rosemary
1 teaspoon olive oil
1 teaspoon salt
¼ teaspoon pepper

- Wash and peel potatoes. Place each potato in the middle of an 8"-square of aluminum foil. With an ice pick or skewer, poke 4 holes ½" deep down the middle of each potato taking care to place them at even intervals.

- Insert rosemary sprigs into holes.

- Drizzle with olive oil, sprinkle with salt and pepper. Wrap in foil.

- Place on grill, using indirect heat and cook 30 to 45 minutes, depending on the size of the potatoes.

Servings: 4

Strawberry-Apple Yogurt

Short of wrapping it in chocolate, this is the best way to get the kids to eat fruit — even big kids like me. —Jack

1 teaspoon butter
1 green apple such as a Granny Smith, peeled, cored, sliced
1 teaspoon lemon juice
1 teaspoon light brown sugar
6 large strawberries, sliced, stems removed
6 ounces vanilla yogurt

- Melt butter in a 1-quart saucepan; add apple, then sprinkle with lemon juice and brown sugar. Cook over medium-high heat about 4 minutes, stirring to coat apples with butter and sugar.
- Add sliced strawberries and cook an additional 2 minutes. Set aside to cool.
- When strawberry-apple mixture has cooled combine with yogurt. Serve chilled in individual glass bowls or parfait glasses.

Servings: 4 to 6

Sweet Potatoes with Orange Drizzle

If you like sweet potatoes, this recipe will make them even tastier. The tangy orange drizzle blends well with natural sugary taste of sweet potatoes, or yams, as my Granny called them. Here's another product the citrus industry should produce and promote – Orange Drizzle. I confess, a snappier name than "orange drizzle" would boost sales. —Jack

3 medium sweet potatoes
1 tablespoon butter, melted
Orange Drizzle (recipe follows)

- Wash sweet potatoes. Prick each 2 or 3 times with a fork.
- Place in microwave oven at least 1 inch apart. Cook on HIGH 9 to 11 minutes or until fork-tender. Cover and let stand 5 minutes. Cut potatoes in half lengthwise. Brush with melted butter. Serve with Orange Drizzle.

Servings: 6

Orange Drizzle

½ cup orange juice
1 teaspoon orange zest
¼ cup balsamic vinegar
¼ cup maple syrup

- Combine all ingredients in a 1-quart saucepan and cook over high heat for 10 to 15 minutes. Cool.

Yield: about 1 cup

Tropical Stars

It's amazing how Mother Nature shapes this unusual fruit. Sliced crosswise it is a shining star and a delicious one at that. And of course, with this recipe, you can make it taste as wonderful as it looks.   *—Jack*

2 star fruit, ends trimmed and sliced crosswise
2 tablespoons lime juice
1 tablespoon light brown sugar
1 tablespoon balsamic vinegar
¼ teaspoon salt
¼ teaspoon white pepper

- Place star fruit slices in a flat 11"-by-7" dish.
- Combine remaining ingredients and pour over fruit. Chill.

Servings: 4 to 6

SOUPS, STEWS AND SANDWICHES

Guacamole Chicken Salad Sandwiches

Not to demean the bird in any way, this new chicken salad is much better than plain old chicken salad. The real difference here is in the addition of avocado — obscurely known as the "butter pear" because the edible portion is like butter, but good for you. Use Hass or Florida avocados for best results. —Jack

1 avocado
¼ cup mayonnaise
2 teaspoons lime juice
1 teaspoon Worcestershire sauce
½ teaspoon salt
¼ teaspoon pepper
1 pound cooked chicken, chopped
Whole wheat bread for toasting

- Cut avocado in half, remove seed and scrape avocado into a large bowl, break up larger pieces but leave a bit chunky.
- Mix in mayonnaise, lime juice, Worcestershire sauce, salt and pepper.
- Add chicken and toss.
- Spread on toasted bread.

Servings: 4 to 6

Y'all Come Avocado Provolone Sandwich

Serve this to guests and chances are it will be a first for them. Cut it into six 2" sandwiches to make a nice hors d'oeuvre or into two 6" sandwiches to make a delicious lunch. —Jack

1 large avocado, peeled and mashed
1 teaspoon lime juice
¼ teaspoon salt
4 ounces provolone cheese, sliced
2 teaspoons spicy brown mustard
1 (12"-section) loaf Cuban bread, sliced lengthwise

- Mash avocado with lime juice and salt.
- Spread mixture on bottom half of Cuban bread. Top with cheese. Spread mustard on cut side of top half and place, mustard side, on top of cheese.
- Cut into six 2" sandwiches.

Servings: 6

Grilled Citrus Flank Sandwiches on Cuban Bread

Flank steak is not a very attractive name for a cow part — not like "filet" or "porterhouse." But it's better than "butt roast." No matter its name, flank steak has wonderful flavor and the two keys to success in making this great sandwich filling are marinating long enough, and slicing it thin enough so that it is supremely tender.

—Jack

1½ pounds flank steak
½ loaf Cuban bread, split lengthwise, cut into sandwich-size pieces
½ cup olive oil
¼ cup soy sauce
¼ cup balsamic vinegar
¼ cup lime juice
¼ cup orange juice
3 cloves garlic, minced
1 tablespoon light brown sugar
1 teaspoon salt
1 teaspoon pepper
Mustard Sauce (recipe follows)

- Combine all ingredients except bread and mustard sauce in a resealable plastic bag.
- Shake to combine ingredients.
- Marinate steak at least 4 hours or overnight in the refrigerator.

Recipe continues on next page ⊃

Grilled Citrus Flank Sandwiches on Cuban Bread

- Using direct heat method, grill steak over medium-hot coals for 4 to 6 minutes on each side or until desired doneness.
- (Remember: The steak will continue to cook for a few minutes after it is removed from the grill.)
- Cut steak diagonally across the grain into very thin slices.
- Serve on Cuban bread with mustard sauce.

Servings: 6

Mustard Sauce

⅓ cup mayonnaise
⅓ cup spicy brown mustard
1 teaspoon Worcestershire sauce
1 teaspoon lime juice

- Combine all ingredients and mix well.

Yield: about ⅔ cup

Sunbeam Bright Lemon Chicken Sandwiches

I'm a sucker for just about all the ingredients that go into this dish. From the soy to the honey, from the provolone to the honey mustard, they all contribute to the great taste. If a chicken must give up his life for our pleasure, this is an honorable way to go.
—Jack

¼ cup extra virgin olive oil
¼ cup lemon juice
2 tablespoons water
1 tablespoon soy sauce
1 tablespoon honey
1 tablespoon spicy brown mustard
½ teaspoon salt
4 skinless boneless chicken breast halves
4 slice provolone cheese
4 hamburger buns
Honey Mustard (recipe follows)

- Whisk together oil, lemon juice, water, soy sauce, honey, mustard and salt. Pour over chicken in a resealable plastic bag. Seal bag and shake to distribute marinade evenly over chicken breasts.

- Refrigerate for several hours or overnight.

- Place the chicken pieces over medium-hot coals and grill that has been sprayed with non-stick cooking spray. Turn chicken several times as it cooks about 30 minutes (approximately 15 minutes per side) or until chicken is done.

- Top with cheese. Serve on buns with honey mustard.

Servings: 4

Recipe continues on next page ⊃

Honey Mustard

**2 tablespoons honey
2 tablespoons spicy brown mustard**

- Whisk honey and mustard together.

Yield: about ¼ cup

Cuban Reuben

This is a fabulous variation of the Reuben sandwich that works perfectly with Cuban bread instead of rye. Had Arthur Reuben, the owner of the New York City deli where this sandwich was invented, been familiar with Cuban bread, he might have named it "Reuven" which is the Spanish version of Reuben. —Jack

Cuban Reuben Sauce (recipe follows)
½ loaf Cuban Bread, sliced lengthwise
¾ pound corned beef
10 ounces Swiss cheese, sliced
1 cup sauerkraut, drained
2 tablespoons butter

- Spread sauce on inside of each bread slice.
- Layer bottom slice of bread with corned beef, cheese and sauerkraut; top with remaining slice of bread.
- Cut into 6 equal sandwiches and press.
- Melt butter in a 10"-frying pan. Press sandwiches with a spatula as they cook, a few minutes on each side.

Servings: 6

Cuban Reuben Sauce

½ cup mayonnaise
1 tablespoon chili sauce
1 tablespoon pickle relish
½ teaspoon lemon juice
¼ teaspoon salt
⅛ teaspoon pepper

- Mix together all ingredients in a small mixing bowl. Refrigerate until ready to use.

Yield: about ¾ cup

Summertime Grilled Burgers

A hamburger, to most folks, is just a ground beef patty, cooked and served with condiments. This version is a "gourmet" burger because so much flavor goes into the patty, you really don't need condiments. You can add cheese and convert them into "gourmet" cheeseburgers. —Jack

1 egg
1 slice white bread, crust removed and torn into
¼-inch pieces
¼ cup finely chopped, sweet onion
1 teaspoon Old Bay® Seasoning
1 teaspoon salt
½ teaspoon freshly ground black pepper
1½ pounds ground beef

- Combine egg and bread in a large mixing bowl. Add onion, Old Bay® Seasoning, salt and pepper. Mix well.
- Add ground meat in small pieces and lightly mix together. Form into 6 patties.
- Grill over medium-high heat for 3 to 5 minutes per side or until the burgers reach the desired degree of doneness.

Servings: 6

Southern (Florida) Lime Chili

There are some risks that come with this recipe. You could be laughed out of the Southwest for suggesting that chili be made with chicken instead of beef. Or asked to leave the South for suggesting chicken rather than pork. But this sure ain't Texas or Alabama. This is Florida!!!! —Jack

**2 pounds bone-in, skinless chicken breasts
1 teaspoon salt
½ teaspoon pepper
1 tablespoon vegetable oil
4 cups water
2 teaspoons olive oil
1 sweet onion, minced
2 cloves garlic, minced
1 medium Anaheim chili, stemmed, seeded and chopped
1 teaspoon ground cumin
1 teaspoon oregano flakes
½ teaspoon coriander
1 (15-ounce) can cannelloni beans, drained
1 cup grated Monterey Jack cheese with jalapenos
2 limes cut into slices
Juice of 1 lime**

- Season the chicken with salt and pepper.
- Heat oil in a 5-quart Dutch oven over medium-high heat. Add chicken and sauté for 4 minutes per side in hot oil.
- Add water and bring to a boil; lower heat to a simmer and cook, covered, for 30 minutes.

Recipe continues on next page ⊃

Southern (Florida) Lime Chili

- Remove chicken from pan with a slotted spoon; reserve liquid. When chicken is cool remove bones and shred meat.
- In a 10"-saute pan, heat olive oil over medium-high heat. When oil sizzles, add onion and cook for about 5 minutes. Add garlic, chili, cumin, oregano and coriander. Cook another 2 minutes, stirring occasionally.
- Add onion mixture to chicken broth along with beans and shredded chicken. Bring to a boil, then lower heat to a simmer, stirring occasionally for about 45 minutes.
- Stir in cheese and sprinkle with lime juice.
- Serve with lime slices on the side for extra flavor and juice.

Servings: 6

Jackson's Black Bean Chili

This is called Jackson's Black Bean Chili because my son, Jackson, created it for a chili cook-off at his school. Good thing he takes after his Mother, because I can't cook a lick. You can tell from the list of ingredients it is a rich and flavorful all-out spicy chili.
—Jack

2 pounds lean ground beef
2 tablespoons vegetable oil
1 medium sweet onion, chopped
1 red bell pepper, seeded and chopped
6 medium garlic cloves, chopped (about 2 tablespoons)
1 tablespoon chili powder
1 teaspoon ground cumin
1 teaspoon ground coriander
1 teaspoon red pepper flakes
1 teaspoon ground oregano
¼ teaspoon cayenne pepper
4 tomatoes, seeded and chopped
1½ cups tomato puree
2 (15-ounce) cans black beans, drained
1 teaspoon salt
2 limes cut into wedges

- Heat oil in a large heavy-bottomed 5-quart soup pot or Dutch oven over medium-high heat.
- Add onions, bell pepper, garlic, chili powder, cumin, coriander, pepper flakes, oregano, and cayenne pepper; cook, stirring occasionally, until vegetables are softened and beginning to brown, 10 to 12 minutes.

Recipe continues on next page ⊃

Jackson's Black Bean Chili

- Increase heat to medium-high and add tomatoes. Cook another 10 to 12 minutes, stirring occasionally.
- Push tomato mixture to one side of pan and add beef; cook, breaking up pieces with wooden spoon, until no longer pink.
- Add beans, tomato puree and salt; reduce heat and simmer covered, stirring occasionally for 45 minutes.
- Remove from heat; serve with lime wedges to be squeezed over bowls of hot chili.

Servings: 6

Family Favorite Vegetable-Beef Soup

This is a Harris family favorite for two reasons: It is a very healthy dish and — far more importantly to Jackson and me — it tastes great. I think it's the big chunk of cheese that crowns it. I like crackers with most soup, but this one needs nothing. It stands alone, though Joy likes it with "frico," which is a kind of baked cheese chip. —Jack

1 tablespoon extra virgin olive oil
1 pound lean ground beef or ground turkey
1 onion, chopped
4 cloves garlic, minced
4 tomatoes, seeds removed, cut into chunks
2 cups chopped cabbage
2 carrots, washed, peeled and diced
1 cup tomato sauce
2 cups chicken broth
1 (4-ounce) chunk Parmigiano-Reggiano cheese
1 (15-ounce) can cannelloni beans, drained (Progresso brand preferred)
1 teaspoon crushed oregano
1 teaspoon salt
1 teaspoon pepper

- Heat oil in a 5-quart Dutch oven or stockpot. Add meat and brown, breaking up pieces with a wooden spoon, until no longer pink. Add onion and garlic, sauté until onions are translucent.

Recipe continues on next page ⊃

Family Favorite Vegetable-Beef Soup

- Add tomatoes, cabbage and carrots along with tomato sauce and chicken broth. Drop in cheese chunk. Lower heat; simmer, covered, for about 1 hour.
- Stir in beans, oregano, salt and pepper. Cook 10 more minutes until all ingredients are heated through.

Servings: 4 to 6

Taste of Tampa
Ham and Bean Soup

If you are new to Florida, particularly the Tampa Bay area, this is a Cuban treat you will come to love. The main ingredient is the garbanzo bean, which you may know by one of its aliases — chickpea or ceci. This Mediterranean staple found its way into Spanish stews and soups, and then into Cuban cuisine, for which I am eternally grateful. —Jack

½ pound dried garbanzo beans
2 quarts water or more if necessary (divided use)
1 chorizo sausage, sliced and removed from its casing
1 ham bone
8 ounces ham, cut into chunks
1 small onion, chopped
3 small potatoes, peeled and cubed
⅛ teaspoon saffron
1 bay leaf
1 teaspoon salt

- Wash garbanzo beans thoroughly, then soak overnight with enough water to cover.
- Drain beans and place in an 8-quart stockpot. Add 1 quart of water along with chorizo, ham bone and ham. Bring to a rapid boil, reduce heat; simmer, covered, 1½ hours. Remove ham bone and discard.
- Add onions, potatoes, saffron, bay leaf and salt.
- Return to a boil, reduce heat; simmer, covered, for 1 hour.
- Remove cover, and then simmer for 15 minutes.
- Remove bay leaf before serving.

Servings: 6

Zellwood Corn Chowder

Zellwood is a town at the heart of the rather modest sweet corn producing region of Florida, and also the home of the annual Sweet Corn Festival. While most Americans think of Kansas or Iowa when they think of corn, here in Florida, we think of Zellwood. The corn is fine and so tasty, you can eat it right off the stalk, but it's even better cooked in this heavenly chowder. —Jack

2 cups fresh corn, cut from the cob (see Note)
2 slices bacon
½ cup chopped sweet onion
¼ cup all-purpose flour
3 cups chicken broth
2 cups chopped potatoes
1 cup diced carrots
½ teaspoon pepper
¾ cup milk
8 ounces sharp Cheddar cheese, shredded

- Cook bacon in a 5-quart Dutch oven over medium-high heat until crisp; add corn and onion. Cook and stir for 2 to 3 minutes.

- Add flour; stir 1 minute then add broth and bring to a boil for 1 minute, stirring once or twice. Add potatoes, carrots and pepper. Simmer, covered for 20 minutes. Remove bacon and discard.

- Gradually stir in milk; cook over medium heat, stirring until mixture is thickened and bubbly. Lower heat, and then add cheese, stirring until melted and well blended.

Servings: 6

Note: *Four medium ears of corn will equal about 2 cups. To cut the corn off the cob, hold the ear upright in a shallow dish, then, with a sharp knife, cut the kernels from the cob in a downward motion.*

DESSERTS

Gator Cake

My wife named this after the national champs in football and basketball, the University of Florida Florida Gators, since it features their colors of orange and blue. As wonderful as this cake tastes, it's hard for my wife to swallow, since she is a Florida State University graduate who cheers on the Seminoles. But it's hard to create a similar cake with their colors of garnet and gold since there's no such thing as a garnet berry. —Jack

2 cups all-purpose flour
1 teaspoon baking soda
½ teaspoon salt
½ teaspoon orange zest
½ cup butter, softened
1 cup sugar
2 eggs
¾ cup milk
¼ cup orange juice
1 cup blueberries, fresh or frozen, thawed
Orange Glaze (recipe follows)

- Preheat oven to 350 degrees F.
- Grease bottom and side of a 9"-round cake pan.
- Mix together flour, baking soda, salt and zest in a large mixing bowl. Set aside. In another large mixing bowl, beat together butter and sugar until light and fluffy. Add eggs one at a time, mixing well after each addition. Stir in milk until well combined.

Recipe continues on next page ⊃

- Then add flour mixture slowly, mixing well as you go. Then stir in orange juice until all is well combined. Gently stir in blueberries.
- Pour batter into prepared pan.
- Bake for 45 minutes or until a toothpick inserted in the center comes out clean. Remove from oven; cool for about 5 minutes. Gently loosen edges with a knife and invert onto a serving plate. Pour glaze over cake. Let cool completely before serving.

Servings: about 8

Orange Glaze

¼ cup orange juice
½ teaspoon orange zest
¼ cup sugar

- Combine all ingredients in a small saucepan. Bring to a boil over medium-high heat. Reduce heat and simmer, about 8 minutes to make light syrup.

Yield: about 1 cup

Kumquat Sweet Tarts

The humble kumquat lives up to its maximum taste potential in this dish. The name is oxymoronic, like jumbo shrimp. It is sweet, and yet tart, but in combo, it is mighty fine.　　　*—Jack*

20 kumquats
½ cup water
4½ graham crackers
1 can sweetened condensed milk
1 egg, slightly beaten
1 teaspoon lime juice

- Preheat oven to 325 degrees F.
- Cut kumquats in half and remove seeds; chop. Place in a pan with water and simmer about 15 minutes or until water has evaporated. Remove from heat.
- Mash kumquats with a potato masher.
- Line an 8"-by-8"-pan with graham crackers.
- Combine kumquats with milk, egg and lime juice in a medium-size bowl. Pour over graham crackers and bake about 8 minutes. Chill.

Servings: 6

Creamy Lemon Pie

Who was the first person who picked a lemon, tasted it, found his face contorting from the wounding acid, then went on to eat it? We owe that anonymous gustatory pioneer a debt of gratitude. Of course, we don't want to forget that intrepid fellow who dared to eat the first egg either. —Jack

1 cup sugar
3 tablespoons cornstarch
¾ cup milk
2 eggs, beaten
4 tablespoons butter, melted
¼ cup lemon juice
1 teaspoon lemon zest
¼ cup light corn syrup
½ cup sour cream
1 (8"-inch) baked pie shell

- Combine sugar and cornstarch in a 2-quart saucepan. Add milk and eggs. Stir in butter, lemon juice and zest. Cook over medium heat, stirring until well thickened.
- Remove from heat; cool.
- Stir in corn syrup and sour cream. Pour into baked pie shell and refrigerate for 1 to 2 hours.

Servings: 6

Lemon Tea Cookies

Girl Scouts, eat your hearts out. This recipe should have been in their cookie mix. It's amazing how something as tart and as bitter as the lemon can be the basis for something as refreshing as these lemon cookies. Joy calls them "tea" cookies, but they taste just as good with other beverages although Lemon Beer Cookies doesn't sound so good — especially for Girl Scouts.   **—Jack**

¾ cup sugar
1½ cups flour
½ teaspoon baking powder
½ cup butter, cold, cut into 1-inch pieces
2 tablespoons lemon juice
1 large egg yolk
Lemon Glaze (recipe follows)

- Combine sugar, flour, and baking powder in a food processor bowl; pulse to combine (about 10 1-second pulses).

- Add butter, pulse until mixture looks like fine cornmeal (about 15 1-second pulses). Add lemon juice and egg yolk. Process until dough begins to form into a ball, 15 to 20 seconds.

- Remove dough and wrap in plastic wrap, refrigerate 1 hour.

- After dough has chilled, preheat oven to 350 degrees F.

- Shape dough into 1" balls and place on a lightly greased baking sheet. Bake for 15 to 18 minutes.

- Remove cookies to wire racks to cool. When cookies have cooled completely, spread each with about ½ teaspoon glaze.

Yield: about 2½ dozen

Recipe continues on next page ⊃

Lemon Glaze

1 tablespoon cream cheese, softened
2 tablespoons lemon juice
1½ cups confectioner's sugar

- Whisk together cream cheese and lemon juice in a small mixing bowl. Add sugar and whisk until smooth.

Yield: about ¾ cup

Nutmeg Ice Cream

Vanilla is the most popular ice cream with chocolate the distant second, followed by butter pecan. You won't find nutmeg on the list, since almost no one has ever tried it. Nutmeg is one of the spices that Columbus was looking for when he sailed from Spain. It is really a tree seed that is covered with a lacy outer membrane. When the nutmeg membrane is dried and ground, it becomes mace. Though it tastes similar to nutmeg, mace-flavored ice cream will probably never catch on.   —Jack

2 cups heavy cream
1 cup whole milk
3 eggs
1 cup sugar
1 teaspoon ground nutmeg
½ teaspoon vanilla
¼ teaspoon salt

- Combine cream, milk, eggs, sugar, nutmeg, vanilla and salt in a heavy saucepan. Cook over low heat, stirring constantly, until mixture coats the back of a spoon, for 10 to 15 minutes.
- Pour into a glass pitcher or 2 quart measuring bowl with a spout. Chill about 1 hour.
- Transfer to ice cream maker and freeze according to manufacturer's directions.

Yield: about 1 quart

Nutty Upside Down Banana Bread

This variation of traditional banana bread tastes so much better. The secret is inversion. Once turned upside down, the banana merges with the butter to give the loaf a special glaze that tastes so amazingly good it is almost sinful. Please note: You will not obtain the same result by cooking it right side up then standing on your head while eating.   —Jack

1½ cups flour
½ teaspoon salt
1 teaspoon baking soda
1 teaspoon cinnamon
¾ cup butter, melted (divided use)
1 cup sugar
2 eggs
2 ripe bananas, mashed
1 tablespoon vanilla
2 tablespoons light brown sugar
½ cup roasted peanuts
1 ripe banana sliced

- Preheat oven to 350 degrees F.
- Whisk together flour, salt, baking soda and cinnamon in a medium-size mixing bowl. Set aside. In another larger mixing bowl, beat ½ cup of the melted butter with sugar and eggs; add mashed bananas and vanilla. Continue beating until well blended.
- Gradually add the banana mixture to dry ingredients. Mix well to form a batter. Set aside.

Recipe continues on next page ⊃

Nutty Upside Down Banana Bread

- Combine brown sugar and peanuts in a small bowl. Stir in remaining ¼ cup of melted butter. Pour into the bottom of a greased 8"-by-8" square baking dish. Top with banana slices.
- Pour banana batter evenly over bananas in the pan.
- Place in the oven and bake for 40 to 45 minutes.
- Cool in pan about 5 minutes. Place platter on top of pan and invert both the pan and the platter. Lift off the pan.

Servings: 6

Sunlight Fluff

Joy got this recipe while she was training to cook for the Florida Department of Natural Resources. It was from the recipe collection of an elderly woman in Pascagoula, Miss., who had cooked for a wealthy family. I imagine that family had a higher cholesterol count than two or three branches of the armed services. I have it only once in a blue moon, but if I were a condemned prisoner, I would request it to top off my last meal. —Jack

½ cup orange juice
1 teaspoon orange zest
1 cup sugar
2 tablespoons butter, melted
3 eggs separated
2 tablespoons flour
⅛ teaspoon salt
1½ cups milk
6 scoops nutmeg ice cream (optional)

- Preheat oven to 350 degrees F.
- Mix together juice, zest, sugar, butter and egg yolks; beat well.
- Whisk together flour and salt in a medium-size mixing bowl. Add sugar mixture. Stir in milk.
- Beat egg whites until they form soft peaks. Fold into sugar mixture.
- Spoon the batter into 6 buttered custard cups. Place cups in a larger pan that has been filled with enough hot water to reach 1 inch up the side of the pan.
- Bake for 45 minutes or until set.
- Serve hot or cold with nutmeg ice cream, if desired.

Servings: 6

Oatmeal Bars
Florida-Style

Great taste doesn't mean a food isn't healthful. This combination of nutritious oatmeal and orange is proof. The oatmeal cookie is tempting on it its own, but topped with delicious orange glaze, it is unforgettable. Joy's orange glaze makes just about anything taste better, even oranges taste better with orange glaze.

—Jack

1 teaspoon orange zest
1 cup butter, softened
1 cup light brown sugar
¾ cup granulated sugar
2 eggs
1 teaspoon vanilla
1½ cups flour
1 teaspoon salt
1 teaspoon soda
½ teaspoon ginger
3 cups old-fashion oatmeal
Orange Glaze (recipe follows)

- Preheat oven to 350 degrees F.
- Combine zest, butter and sugars in a medium-size mixing bowl; add eggs and vanilla and beat well until light and fluffy.
- In another mixing bowl, combine flour, salt, baking soda and ginger; add to butter and sugar mixture. Stir in oats and mix well.
- Bake in an ungreased 13"-by-9"-inch pan for 30 to 35 minutes.

Recipe continues on next page ⊃

- While still warm drizzle with Orange Glaze. Cut into 16 rectangular shaped bars.

Servings: 16

Orange Glaze

2 tablespoons orange juice
1 cup confectioner's sugar

- Whisk ingredients together until sugar dissolves.

Yield: about ½ cup

Tropical Pizza

No pizza delivery guy will come to your home with anything like this in a cardboard box. Inside that box you'd find traditional pizza, which had its beginnings in Naples. That's Naples, Italy, not Naples, Florida. Naples, Florida could easily provide the ingredients for this pizza that is heavy on oranges and strawberries. Pity those folks in the Mediterranean. —Jack

½ cup butter
½ cup sugar
1 egg yolk
½ teaspoon vanilla
1½ cups all-purpose flour
1 teaspoon baking soda
Strawberry Cream Cheese (recipe follows)
3 cups strawberries, stems removed and sliced
Orange Sauce (recipe follows)

- Preheat oven to 350 degrees F.
- Beat butter and sugar together until creamy. Add egg yolk and vanilla; beat well. Whisk together flour and baking soda; add to butter mixture. Beat well. Pat dough into a 12" pizza pan and chill for 15 minutes.
- Place on center rack in oven and bake for 18 to 20 minutes.
- Spread Strawberry Cream Cheese over cooled crust, and then arrange sliced strawberries on top. Pour Orange Sauce over pizza and chill.

Servings: 6

Recipe continues on next page ↻

Strawberry Cream Cheese

1 (3-ounce) package cream cheese, softened
2 tablespoons confectioner's sugar
¼ cup strawberries, stems removed and sliced

• Beat all ingredients together until smooth.

Yield: about ¾ cup

Orange Sauce

1 cup orange juice
2 tablespoons lemon juice
½ cup sugar
1/8 teaspoon salt
1 tablespoon cornstarch

• Combine orange juice and lemon juice in a 1-quart saucepan. Combine sugar, salt and cornstarch together in a measuring cup; whisk into juices and bring to a boil. Boil 3 to 4 minutes, stirring occasionally. Remove from heat and cool.

Yield: about 1½ cups

Peanut Butter-Banana Parfait

If you've never tried the combination of peanut butter and banana, you've missed a great gustatory delight. I discovered the combo in sandwiches, which are maybe the driest albeit yummiest sandwiches ever. The take-away is this: Everything tastes better with peanut butter — jelly, sweet pickles, and especially bananas.   —Jack

2 ripe bananas
2 tablespoons lemon juice
¼ cup brown sugar
¼ cup smooth peanut butter
¼ cup honey
1 pint vanilla or nutmeg ice cream

* Combine all ingredients, except the ice cream, in a blender or food processor and blend until smooth. Spoon ice cream into parfait or dessert dishes, spoon sauce over top.

Servings: 6

Flamingo Pink Lime Pie

My previous all-time favorite dessert was Key Lime Pie – but then I tasted Flamingo Pink Lime Pie and my world changed. Joy tells me that the main difference is the red food coloring, otherwise it delivers the same wonderful tangy-sweet taste of Key Lime Pie. I reckon we really do eat with our eyes and that visual impact changes everything. —Jack

Crust:
1½ cups graham cracker crumbs
¼ cup butter, melted

Filling:
½ cup Key lime juice
1 (3-ounce) package cream cheese, softened
1 (14-ounce) can sweetened condensed milk
1 large egg
3 to 4 drops red food coloring

- Preheat oven to 325 degrees F.
- Mix crumbs and butter together; press firmly into a 9-inch pie pan.
- Refrigerate crust while making filling.
- Beat cream cheese in a medium-size mixing bowl with an electric mixer until smooth and creamy. Beat in milk, egg and lime juice. Add food coloring, mixing well until color is uniform. Pour into prepared crust and spread evenly. Bake about 15 minutes.
- Cool and refrigerate until well chilled, about 2 hours.

Servings: 6

Honey Berry Cakes

In wintertime, Central Florida beekeepers bring bee colonies to pollinate strawberry fields. Gathering strawberry blossom pollen, the bees produce a strawberry honey that's quite distinctive. However, Joy circumvents the process by simply combining the strawberries with whatever honey is available in the store. Any way you look at it, it's a dish that is bee-witching. —Jack

1 teaspoon orange juice
1 teaspoon orange zest
1 medium apple, peeled, cored and chopped
2 cups flour
1 teaspoon baking powder
½ teaspoon salt
½ teaspoon cardamom
¼ cup butter, softened
1 cup sugar
1 egg, beaten
½ cup buttermilk
Strawberry Honey (recipe follows)

- Preheat oven to 350 degrees F.
- Sprinkle orange juice and zest over apple slices in a small bowl. Set aside. In a different bowl, whisk together flour, baking powder, salt and cardamom. Set aside.
- Beat together butter and sugar until light and fluffy in a medium-size mixing bowl. Beat in egg and when it is well incorporated, stir in buttermilk. Add reserved flour mixture and stir until dry ingredients are just moistened.
- Stir in apple mixture.

Recipe continues on next page ↪

Honey Berry Cakes

- Spray two 12-cup muffin pans or one 24-cup muffin pan with non-stick baking spray. Divide batter evenly among baking cups. Place on middle rack of the oven and bake for 25 minutes or until a wooden pick inserted in the center of a muffin comes out clean.
- Remove muffins from pan and set on wire rack to cool slightly.
- Serve warm with Strawberry Honey.

Yield: 2 dozen muffins

Strawberry Honey

2 cups fresh strawberries, stems removed and sliced
1 cup honey (divided use)
¼ cup orange juice

- Combine strawberries, ½ cup honey and orange juice in a 1-quart saucepan. Heat to boiling over medium-high heat; reduce heat and simmer for about 15 minutes. Stir in remaining honey. Remove from heat and cool.

Yield: about 2 cups

Strawberry Coffee Cake

You'd think a coffee cake would be made with "coffee" — but coffee isn't in the batter or the frosting or the crumb. It's a cake to be served with coffee, but unlike a dessert cake, coffee cake is just a humble, homey sweet treat that goes great with coffee or any other beverage you care to serve. —Jack

1 tablespoon sugar
2 cups fresh strawberries, stems removed, thinly sliced
1½ cups flour
1 teaspoon baking powder
½ teaspoon baking soda
¼ teaspoon salt
1 cup sugar
½ cup butter, melted and cooled
¾ cup vanilla yogurt
1 egg

- Preheat oven to 350 degrees F.
- Sprinkle the tablespoon of sugar over the sliced strawberries; set aside. Combine flour, baking powder, soda, salt and sugar in a medium-size bowl; set aside. Whisk together butter and yogurt until well combined in a large mixing bowl, then whisk in egg. Add flour mixture and mix well. Fold in strawberries. Grease bottom and side of an 8"-square baking pan. Pour batter into pan and smooth top. Place in oven and bake for 45 minutes.

Servings: 6

Chilled Strawberry Torta

"Torta" can be an omelet, a sandwich, a bread or a cake, depending on which country defines it. Joy has made her tort into a layered delight with simple ingredients cleverly arranged. This is so easy, and so good, especially when the strawberries are in from the strawberry capital of the universe, Plant City, Florida. — Jack

3 cups strawberries, stems removed and sliced
¾ cup sugar
¼ teaspoon nutmeg
1 (9"-by-9") frozen puff pastry sheet, thawed (see Note)

- Preheat oven to 400 degrees F.
- Combine strawberries, sugar and nutmeg in a 2-quart saucepan; cook over medium heat for 15 minutes, stirring occasionally. The mixture will become very wet as the strawberries release their juices.
- While the berries are cooking, cut the puff pastry into 3 strips that are 9"-by-3" each. Place the strips on an ungreased baking sheet and bake them for 10 to 15 minutes or until golden.
- Remove from oven and place one of the strips on the bottom of a 9"-by-5"-by-3" loaf pan. Spoon ⅓ of the cooked berries over the pastry. Do this 2 more times, ending with berries. Lower heat to 350 degrees and bake for 25 minutes.
- Chill before serving.

Servings: 6

Note: *This recipe can also be prepared by substituting buttered bread for the pastry as follows: Butter 9 slices of crustless bread. Use 3 slices per layer of pastry. Place the bread butter side down in the pan.*

NOTES

NOTES

THE AUTHORS

About Joy

Joy Harris was born in Tripoli, Libya (her father was in the Air Force), but grew up in Panama City, Florida. She graduated with a Bachelor's degree in Home Economics Education from Florida State University and later obtained a Master's Degree in Education as well as Psychology. Joy taught Home Economics for six years before taking a job with the state of Florida as a Marketing Specialist promoting Florida seafood. She has presented numerous cooking demonstrations appearing on a variety of television and radio shows. At one of those on-air appearances Joy met Jack, and as Jack would say "Holy guacamole!" The rest is history.

About Jack

Jack's hometown is Logan, West Virginia, where he worked at a local radio station, WVOW. He attended Davidson College and graduated from West Virginia University with a Bachelor's degree in History. From 1970 until present Jack has worked extensively in the Tampa Bay radio and television market. Jack has been a member of the broadcast team of the Tampa Bay Buccaneers for many years, as well as the Storm and the Outback Bowl. He has been a host of several number one rated radio and television shows and is currently co-host of AM Tampa Bay on FOX radio 970 WFLA. "Cracker" Jack also served as honorary Mayor of Ybor City and is the author of "Jack Harris Unwrapped: Ruminations, Recipes and Robust Raillery." Jack is married to Joy. Together they have a son Jackson who is also an avid gastronome.